The Rainbow Club

Library of Congress Control Number: 2007001023

ISBN 978-1-59566-393-1

Written by Annette Aubrey
Edited by Sarah Medina
Designed by Alix Wood
Illustrated by Patrice Barton
Consultancy by David Hart

Publisher Steve Evans
Creative Director Zeta Davies
Senior Editor Hannah Ray

Printed and bound in China

The Rainbow Club

Annette Aubrey

Illustrated by
Patrice Barton

QEB Publishing

QEB

Chloe and Tommy were

best friends.

They loved to find new things to do.

"Tomorrow, let's make a Green Team when we go on our trip to the zoo!

4

"Let's put on our green clothes tomorrow
and be friendly with everyone who
acts just like us and wears just green,
who would never, ever wear blue!"

On the bus, the children were excited.
There was Nathan and Lily and Zach,
and Catherine and Lauren and Ethan,
all carrying their lunch in their bags.

They'd all dressed in different colors,
from yellow to red to black.

All the colors of the rainbow,

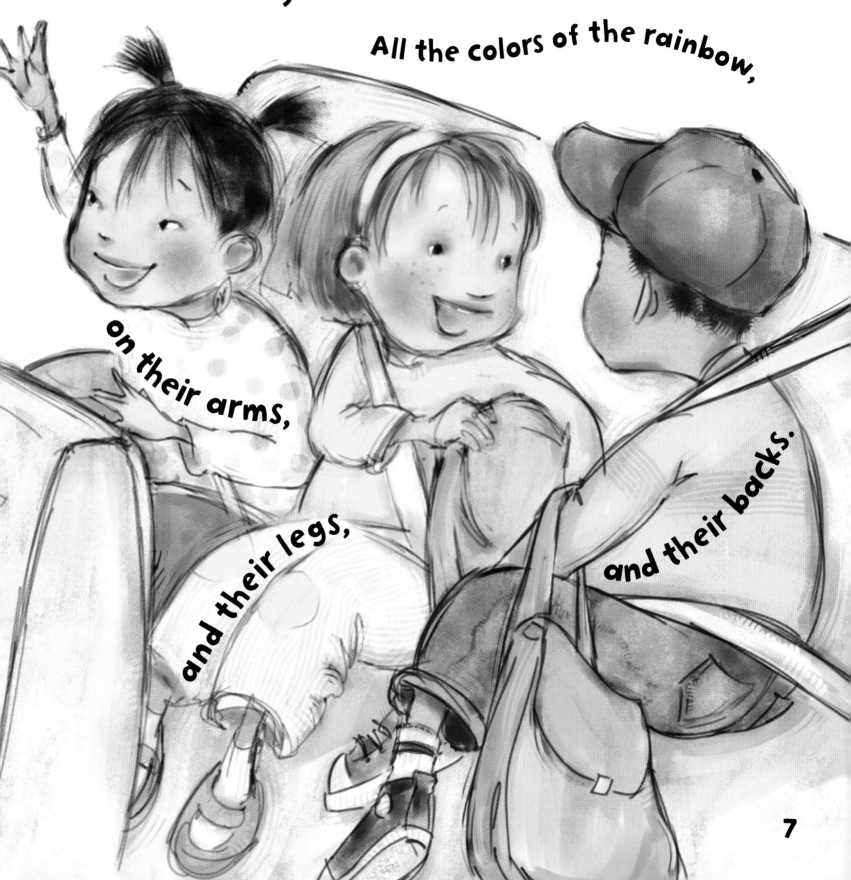

on their arms,

and their legs,

and their backs.

The kids wearing green started cheering
when Chloe and Tommy did say,

"We're glad that we're so very special.
We each wore our green clothes today!

"We'll never wear blue!
It just wouldn't do!
Just what would our green friends say?
And now that we're on the Green Team,

it's only with **Greenies** we'll play."

9

Some children, like Susie and Ollie
and David and Maya and Brad,
who weren't to be seen
    wearing anything green,

felt left out and **terribly** sad.

10

But the ones who felt really awful,
the ones who felt truly bad,
were the kids wearing blue
            (there were quite a few).
They were hurt and embarrassed

                and **mad!**

And it was strange to see what happened,
quite the weirdest thing you have seen.
The children who wore other colors
tried hard to find ways to be green.

They turned their backs on the blue kids,
so that they could join the Green Team.

We won't play with you.
You're just too uncool.
You're not one of us!

They were
mean!

And so it is true that the zoo trip
got off to a very bad start.
And rather than playing together,
friends were tearing each other apart.

It was awful to see and hear it!
How could it have gone quite so far?
The things friends were saying and doing

were **horrible**

and **hurtful**

and **hard**.

Then, in stepped a classmate named Ella.
She spoke in a voice clear and true.

Please, just forget all of this nonsense
about who should wear
green or wear blue.

It's what is inside us that really matters!
Who cares what we look like or do?
We should remember that we are all special,
and should be kind to each other, too.

Chloe and Tommy thought for a while,
then said to the kids from their school,

"We have to admit that

we've got it

all wrong.

We're the ones who
are really uncool.

"To hurt others because they are different
is unkind and horrible and cruel.
Far better to include everybody

in a **new club**

that clearly is cool!"

The children on the trip all sighed with relief
when they heard what the Greens had to say.
And everyone smiled as they each did agree,

"It's true that we're really OK!

"Deep down, we really do want to
be friends with each other and play."

And so the **Rainbow Club** was started,
right there on the zoo trip that day.

You see, children are very smart.
If they look, they really can see
all the good things there are in each other.
If you asked them, they'd surely agree.

22

On the inside, we're the same as each other.
We all think, and we laugh, and we cry.
We're much more alike than we're different.

And we can be friends if we try!

NOTES FOR PARENTS AND TEACHERS

- Look at the front cover of the book together. Talk about the picture. Can the children guess what the book is going to be about?
- Turn to pages 4 and 5, where Chloe and Tommy form a "Green Team." Ask the children if they have ever made up new clubs or activities. If so, were they open to everyone, or were they just for a few people?
- Talk about how the children are different on pages 6 and 7. Ask the readers if their friends always wear the same clothes. Ask them in what other ways people might be different from each other.
- On pages 8 and 9, Chloe and Tommy announce the new club to the other children. Ask the children how the other children on the trip might feel about this. What would the children think, if they were there?
- Talk about the different feelings that the children have on pages 10 and 11. Ask the readers why they think that the children who were not wearing green felt left out. Why was it worse for the children who were wearing blue?
- Read pages 12 and 13 together again. Discuss what is happening. Ask the readers why the other children want to be part of the Green Team. How do they think the "blue" children are feeling? Point out that it is unkind to leave other people out and to say mean things to them. Say that this is bullying, and that bullying hurts people very badly.
- Turn to pages 14 and 15. Talk about different ways that people bully others—through their actions and through their words. Have the children ever seen someone being bullied?
- On pages 16 and 17, Ella confronts the Green Team. Discuss with the readers that Ella is very brave to do this. Say that she must have felt nervous, but that she stood up to the bullies anyway, because she believes that bullying is wrong. Ask the children what other things they could do to stop bullying. Suggest different ideas, such as asking a trusted adult for help. Tell your children that no one has to put up with being bullied.
- On pages 18 and 19, Chloe and Tommy admit that they were wrong to bully the children who were different from them. Ask the readers why Chloe and Tommy now think that they are the ones who are "uncool."
- Read pages 20 and 21 together again. Point out that the children on the zoo trip were relieved that the bullying had stopped. Often, children get caught up in bullying because they are following a leader. Ask the readers if they think it is right to bully someone just because someone else is a bully. Suggest that they can be brave, like Ella, and stay away from bullies.
- Discuss the ideas about equality and mutual respect on pages 22 and 23. Ask your children to think about children who they do not know very well. Do they think they can be friends with them? If not, why not? Explore the idea that people are "more alike than different." Does this change their mind?